SOFT SKILLS DEVELOPMENT:

Belief

Dr. S. L. Young

Table of Contents

Soft Skills Development Summary

Belief is an important tool, but it's something that's too often underutilized. An ability to believe in a concept, a goal, yourself, and other considerations are important steps toward the achievement of a desired outcome. Therefore, individuals must take actions to improve their belief system to maximize opportunities to achieve ongoing success.

Soft Skills Developments provide individuals with information that focuses on the delivery of valuable and actionable content without a significant time investment.

This Soft Skills Development addresses the:
- Reasons that belief is important
- Components of belief
- Impact of not having belief
- Benefits of having belief
- Tools to move past doubts, fears, and worries toward actionable goals
- Use of belief for an individual's advantage

Enjoy!

"Belief"

Belief is something that individuals have difficulty with for many different reasons. Beliefs can be a challenge due to someone's views, others' beliefs (forced or not), fear, doubt, worrying about others' opinions, and more. The good news is that even some of the most successful people struggle with having belief. Therefore, challenges with it aren't limited to those who haven't yet experienced their desired success.

The hardest part of getting started is convincing yourself to begin. If taking the first step toward a goal or an objective is the hardest part, then... why don't individuals just get going and do it? The reason (many times) is that individuals limit their potential success(es) due to perceived doubts, fears, and worries about themselves or from others.

If the worst thing that can happen is that someone falls short of their goals or experiences a little humiliation, then the good news is... nobody has died of humiliation, and you probably won't be the first.

By using effective strategies to eliminate barriers to beliefs, individuals can actively pursue their dreams without unnecessary burdens or self-imposed limitations.

Failure is normal and an essential part of the growth process. Remember that there's always value in the journey, even if the outcome isn't as wanted or expected. Therefore, individuals should actively pursue their dreams and use their belief(s) as the fuel to help themselves (and sometimes others) to achieve the most that can possibly be achieved during their life's journey.

"Belief" – What Is It?

Belief:

- is a feeling that X is worth doing

- drives action

- is needed to sustain the energy required to continue to make progress

- helps individuals take the initial step(s) toward a goal

- keeps individuals moving forward despite overwhelming odds, setbacks, or challenges

- and much more

For individuals to invest their time, energy, and effort, there must be a "belief" that something of value will be received (e.g., knowledge, enjoyment, distraction). Otherwise, their time will be directed elsewhere.

Consequently, individuals won't usually TEE OFF[1]

---

[1] Read the article "Belief: An Underutilized Tool" in the Appendix on page 64 for additional information about this topic.

to work on a goal or objective until there's a desire to use their (T)ime, (E)nergy, and (E)ffort (O)n (F)ulfilling (F)antasies (which is otherwise known as dreams).

<u>What Are Your Barriers to Having "Belief?"</u>

List three barriers that prevent you from having or maximizing your beliefs.

1.

2.

3.

"Belief" Challenges

Challenges associated with the development of someone's beliefs:

- Fear of the unknown

- Doubts about someone's capabilities

- Worrying about others' opinions

- Personal beliefs

- Others' beliefs (forced or not)

- Past experiences

- Fear of success

- Fear of failure

- And more

Challenges related to belief can be considered or experienced while pursuing a task, an activity, an opportunity, a goal, or an objective. Therefore, a method to conquer challenges to someone's beliefs is to understand that these types of issues exist and make a conscious decision to move forward anyway. Otherwise, opportunities to achieve your desires or goals might be lost.

Reasons for Having "Belief"

Belief is required to purposely:

- Complete a task

- Finish an activity

- Achieve a goal

- Accomplish an objective

Simply put... belief ignites the fuel that helps individuals make progress sometimes despite overwhelming odds.

Components of "Belief"

The components of "belief:"

- <u>Concept</u> – Is this considered to be true?

- <u>Consideration</u> – Is this true for me?

- <u>Convenience</u> – Is this true for me at this moment?

Evaluation of the Components of "Belief"

- Concept – Is this considered to be true?

  o Something that's applied and generally accepted as true

- Consideration – Is this true for me?

  o Something that's a possibility, but there may or may not be a willingness to act

- Convenience – Is this true for me at this moment?

  o Something that will be done only if it meets a goal or an objective (personal or otherwise)

Application of "Belief" Components (Example #1)

- <u>Concept</u> – Something that's applied and generally accepted as true

  - o Individuals should pursue a college degree.

- <u>Consideration</u> – Something that's a possibility, but there may or may not be a willingness to act

  - o If I go to college, then I might have additional career options.

- <u>Convenience</u> – Something that will be done only if it meets a goal or an objective (personal or otherwise)

  - o The company I work for will pay for my tuition, which otherwise I couldn't afford to pay.

Application of "Belief" Components
(Example #2)

- <u>Concept</u> – Something that's applied and generally accepted as true

    o Unethical behavior is wrong and should be resolved quickly.

- <u>Consideration</u> – Something that's a possibility, but there may or may not be a willingness to act

    o Someone observes unethical behavior and decides whether to report it.

- <u>Convenience</u> – Something that will be done only if it meets a goal or an objective (personal or otherwise)

    o Someone is aware of unethical behavior but doesn't report it because it might negatively impact them. Otherwise, the unethical behavior would be reported.

Application of "Belief" Components
(Example #3)

- <u>Concept</u> – Something that's applied and generally accepted as true

    o Becoming an author is a recognized accomplishment.

- <u>Consideration</u> – Something that's a possibility, but there may or may not be a willingness to act

    o Someday I want to write a book.

- <u>Convenience</u> – Something that will be done only if it meets a goal or an objective (personal or otherwise)

    o I had an experience that changed my life. Now, I want to share it with others.

Impact of Not Having "Belief"

Belief can hold individuals back due to:

- a lack of motivation;

- being burdened by doubts, fears, and worries;

- being hesitant about taking the first step toward an opportunity;

- being comfortable in their current situation;

- an unwillingness to push themselves;

- not achieving their potential.

Benefits of Having "Belief"

Belief can be used to:

- Make a change

- Make a difference

- Do something better

- Drive a new idea

- Move past a challenge

- Explore a new idea

- And much more

Simply put… "belief" drives progress.

Develop a Growth Mindset

Failure isn't a destination! Instead, setbacks should be used as opportunities to learn, for growth, and to experience self-discovery.

Consider the following:

- What didn't go well?

- What did I learn from it?

- What could be done better in the future?

- What skills should be developed to maximize my opportunities?

By actively taking action to address setbacks, it begins to create a process to develop resilience and perseverance to achieve other goals.

Maintain a positive mindset to drive your beliefs.

Remember… *there's always value in the journey, even if the outcome isn't as wanted or expected*, as lessons can be learned from every experience.

Who Do You Want to Be?

List three adjectives that describe the person you want to become.

1.

2.

3.

"Belief" Is Important Because...

Fear can compel you to action or cause you to be stifled from achieving personal greatness.[2]

Beliefs impact someone's:

- Morals, principals, and faith
- Mindset, including their health
- Determinations about whether something is worth doing or beginning
- Ego and self-esteem
- Perceptions about themselves or their abilities
- Daily activities and interactions
- Willingness to obtain assistance or advice
- Decisions
- Desires to drive their future success

---

[2] Young, S. L. It's a Crazy World... Learn From It: Part I – Taking Care of Me. Beyond SPRH, LLC, 2012 - 2014, 2023 - 2024, p. 49. Print.

Don't Worry Too Much

Believe it's possible without worrying too much. Otherwise, your potential success(es) can be impacted before you ever get started.

Minimize the impacts created by unnecessary:

- Fears
- Doubts
- Worries

An Example

- I wrote my first book in 2012.

- Later in 2012, I wrote two more books.

- I wrote three books in 2013.

- Sales didn't happen as quickly as I wanted, but I read an article in 2012 that provided advice for authors to keep writing regardless of the numbers of books sold.

- This guidance was important because even if my initial books didn't sell quickly. Then, a later book might and could drive sales for past publications.

- As sales increased, my books were used in additional environments (e.g., high schools, college programs, diversion programs).

- None of this would have been possible without me having "belief".

My beliefs kept me moving forward, as I believed in the messages in my books. Also, I believed that later books would bring awareness for my work.

<u>Consideration #1</u>

Believe that your efforts will add value (even if there aren't immediate results), because if you don't "believe" in your work...

Then, why should anyone else?!

Exercise

Fill in the blanks with the adjectives that describe the individual you want to be (reference page 22).

- I am _____

- I am _____

- I am _____

Change Starts with You

Change who you are by first determining who or what you want to be.

<u>Note:</u> Read the article "Are You Really Who You Think You Are?" in the Appendix on page 74.

Develop a Plan to Overcome
Your Barriers to "Belief"

What impacts your willingness to fully "believe" in your ability to achieve your goals and objectives?
- *Consider… What's stopping you?*

1.

2.

3.

What are the reasons for these barriers?
- *Consider… Why is it stopping you?*

1.

2.

3.

What actions will be taken to eliminate the barriers?
- *Consider... What will you do to move forward?*

1.

2.

3.

When will the corresponding actions be taken to eliminate these barriers?
- *Consider... When will your plan be implemented?*

1.

2.

3.

Self-Talk: What Is It?

<u>Self-Talk</u> – an intentional conversation someone has with themself to help direct their thoughts, which could lead to a new attitude or a change in a previous belief

Self-Talk: Why Is It Important?

A self-talk is important because it:

- Helps to override negative thoughts or comments from others

- Assists with the development of positive thoughts and intentions

- Changes attitudes or past "beliefs"

- Develops "beliefs" by defining the things that are important

- Transforms thoughts into "beliefs" via repetition

- Builds confidence

- Communicates desired future behavior

- Drives meaningful action

Self-Talk: By the Numbers

A self-talk can be impactful and a powerful tool if it's repeated throughout the day.

If it's said aloud, then the brain processes it multiple times because:

- It's thought
- It's spoken
- It's heard
- It's processed

For example:

- If it's said once a day, repeated three (3) times.

    o It's processed twelve (12) times.

- If it's said twice a day, repeated six (6) times.

    o It's processed twenty-four (24) times.

- If it's said three times a day, repeated nine (9) times.

    o It's processed thirty-six (36) times.

Power of a Self-Talk

A self-talk is an underused and a valuable tool to program or reprogram your thoughts and "beliefs."

My First Self-Talk

"I am a clear, concise, confident communicator."

This self-talk (repeated aloud many times to myself) helped to change this naturally shy person into a dynamic speaker.

My Past Self-Talk

"You're wasting time doing stupid things and not being the person that you're meant to be."

Before I realized or achieved my future potential and successes, this self-talk envisioned that I was willing, capable, and driven to do more meaningful work.

My Current Self-Talk

"I'm a superstar!"

Why should anyone think any differently about themselves?

If you want to be the best (which doesn't mean perfection), _your self-talk_ should be nothing less than that which _directs your mind toward the most success_.

Your Self-Talk

The sentences completed in the exercise "I am _____." (reference page 27) can be used as your self-talk or the basis to create a more in-depth self-talk.

Homework

Repeat each of your "I am _____." self-talk sentences at least three times in the morning, afternoon, and at night.

If it's difficult to use all three sentences at the same time, then select one to use for a while and then select another.

"Belief's" Power

Your desire for change must be greater than your desire to remain in the same position. In other words, you must really "believe" that your goals and objectives are important, possible, purposeful, and achievable.

"Belief" can provide the fuel to help propel meaningful progress without any concerns about the challenges that might need to be overcome to achieve success.

Secret to Success

- <u>Believe</u> – it's possible

- <u>Hope</u> – allows you to move forward based on a "belief" that something better is ahead

- <u>Act</u> – good things (usually) don't happen unless time, energy, effort, and focus are directed toward a goal

Redefine "no" to "new orientation." If someone tells you "no" and you still want more, then redirect your energy toward another focal point that will get you closer to your "yes."

Conquer Fear – Maximize "Belief"

Use these Ps to conquer your fear(s) and maximize your belief(s):

- Patience

- Passion

- Planning

- Persistence

- Perseverance

- Pain

- Perspective

- Purpose

- Positivity

- And if you "believe" … there's always prayer

Maximize Your "Belief"

The value of "belief" is that:

- It helps you move forward toward the unknown.

- It isn't required to move forward, but it can increase your confidence and determination to continue.

- It can help you move forward despite overwhelming odds, setbacks, or challenges.

- It aids in the making, development, and achievement of dreams.

- It supports your efforts to achieve your personal greatness.

Difference between faith and belief:

- <u>Faith</u> – powers the strength to begin

- <u>Belief</u> – provides positive affirmations that something is possible to achieve

Remove Barriers to Your "Belief" System

An ability to "truly believe" requires an ability to:

- Manage fears

- Overcome doubts

- Minimize worries

Each of these (if not properly addressed and managed) is an unnecessary and preventable barrier to maximizing your "beliefs," along with achieving successes.

Test Your Resolve

Questions that can be used to test your resolve:

- Why is this important?

- Why should this be done?

    o This isn't necessarily the same as the reason that it's important.

- What or who could be impacted?

    o If it's done; if it's not done.

- What might be lost, missed, or compromised if this isn't done?

    o This is the opportunity cost (*the value of doing activity X versus activity Y*).

- What are the short-term and long-term costs?

    o This also includes the opportunity cost.

- What are the short-term and long-term risks?

    o Expected and not as likely.

- What are the short-term and long-term benefits?

    o Expected and not as likely.

- What might others think about the effort?

    o Others' thoughts shouldn't necessarily prevent your progress. Instead, it should be used to reexamine your plans and prepare thoughtful responses to any objections.
    o Others' noes shouldn't prevent you from continuing to pursue your positive dreams, goals, and desires.
    o Lack of support, doubts, and resistance experienced by others could be a test of your resolve. If you're willing to easily give-up, then you probably weren't fully committed. Therefore, you might consider exploring other options.
    o If there are strong negative reactions to gain support, then redefine the word "no" to "new orientation." Then, be ready to develop different strategies to achieve your dreams.

What could be learned from the effort?

- o Sometimes value is derived from an unplanned journey, even if the outcome isn't as wanted or expected.

- What's the worst thing that could happen?

    - o It's normally less than might be expected.
    - o Remember… no one has ever died from humiliation, and you won't be the first.

- What will be achieved by the effort?

- Considering all these questions, is it worth your time, energy, effort, or the cost (real or perceived) to proceed?

Ask Yourself

- Is X worth your time, energy, attention, focus, effort, or anything else of importance?

- Is X more valuable than your other options?

  - If so, proceed.
    - Also, ask yourself, "Why am I doing the other things?"

  - If not, continue to work on the other things.

"Belief" is an important factor in moving forward, along with its close associates of time management and prioritization.

Consideration #2

- Too much time is spent worrying about others' opinions, especially from those who aren't known, don't matter, or haven't done the things you're trying to do.

- There are a lot of critics, including ourselves. However, the most important critic (if it's positive and constructive) is "you."
    o Be your biggest fan and cheerleader!

- The focus should be on delivering excellence versus perfection, because perfection isn't normally achievable.

<u>Key Message</u>

If fear is allowed to get in your way, then you're more likely to continue to be the individual you are today without becoming who you could be during your life's journey.

Jump-Start Your "Beliefs"

Strive for excellence and not perfection:

- Perfection is generally not attainable as things can always be done better.

- Excellence is achievable because it's the best you can do at a particular moment.

Seeking perfection can negatively impact your "beliefs" and motivations. Therefore, strive for excellence, as it helps to build confidence.

Perfect may be the view from your mother's eye, but perfection isn't part of everyday life.[3]

---

[3] Young, S. L. It's a Crazy World... Learn From It: Part III – Keeping It Going. Beyond SPRH, LLC, 2012 - 2014, 2023 - 2024, pp. 24. Print.

"Belief": The Beginning

- Even if you don't know if it can be done, move forward anyway.

- Understand that each subsequent step gets you closer to your desired outcome.

- Learn from past experiences to be better the next time.

- Continue to adjust along the way.

"Belief": Parting Thought #1

You can't be anything you want, but you can work toward anything you want. Then, if you fall short of your goal(s), then there's still value in the journey.

"Belief": Parting Thought #2

At times, individuals must step-away, step-back, or step-up:

- Step-away if you gave it your best and you don't have more to give

- Step-back to regroup to try it again later

- Step-up to make a positive difference for yourself and others

"Belief": Parting Thought #3

Do It For You[4]:

- Do it for you, even though others may question it

- Do it for you, while others don't understand it

- Do it for you, while others may challenge it

- Do it for you, even if you don't completely believe it's possible

- Do it for you, especially if your effort will also help others

- Do it for you, because positive change starts with you

---

[4] Young, S. L. It's a Crazy World... Learn From It: Part IV – The Journey Continues. Beyond SPRH, LLC, 2013 - 2014, 2023 - 2024, p. 86. Print.

"Belief": Parting Thought #4

- <u>Your beliefs yesterday…</u>

    o Are important to get prepared for something today

- <u>Your beliefs tomorrow…</u>

    o Will help you to continue your progress toward success

- <u>Your beliefs today…</u>

    o Allow you to be the best possible you at this moment… and this is within your immediate control

"Belief": Parting Thought #5

Remain in the moment, keep your mind focused on current work, and most importantly enjoy the journey of discovery.

"Belief": Parting Thought #6

<u>Perspective</u>[5]:

- The past – Is over

- The present – Is now

- The future – Hasn't happened

****

- There's nothing that can be done to change the past

- The present is within your control

- Creating and executing a plan (now) will affect your future

---

[5] Young, S. L. It's a Crazy World...Learn From It: Part I – Taking Care of Me. Arlington, Virginia: Beyond SPRH, LLC, 2012 – 2014, 2023 - 2024, page 76. Print.

"Belief": Parting Thought #7

<u>Roadmap to Success</u>[6]...

- Dream (of possibilities)

- Desire (to do more)

- Determination (fueled by belief)

- Drive (to get through the tough times)

- Decisiveness (to make decisions)

- Dedication (to achieve the dream)

---

[6] Young, S. L. It's a Crazy World...Learn From It: Part I – Taking Care of Me. Arlington, Virginia: Beyond SPRH, LLC, 2012 – 2014, 2023 - 2024, page 16. Print.

"Belief": Parting Thought #8

Pursue Unrestricted Sustained Happiness[7]

- Push yourself to complete a task

- Push yourself beyond your past

- Push yourself to explore many doors

- Push yourself to achieve even more

- Push yourself to get a different view

- Push yourself to become your best you

---

[7] Young, S. L. It's a Crazy World… Learn From It: Part IV – The Journey Continues. Beyond SPRH, LLC, 2013 - 2014, 2023 - 2024, p. 84. Print.

<u>Always Remember to...</u>

- Believe it's possible

- Enjoy the journey

- Be _your_ best!

Soft Skills Development: Parting Thoughts

An ability to maximize "belief" requires individuals to be willing to think about things differently, explore new options, and never give-up on trying different solutions.

Everyone experiences challenges with "belief." However, if individuals develop skills to adjust their perspectives to think about the positives versus the negatives, then it will be easier to conquer any doubts, fears, or worries.

Perfection isn't realistic but being your best is achievable, and it's within your control. Therefore, if the outcome isn't as expected, then take as much as possible from the experience and use the knowledge to be better the next time.

Life is about cumulative moments. Therefore, focus on the positives, quickly forget the negatives, and always believe in the possibilities. This way your maximum effort can always be applied toward the pursuit of your dreams, goals, and objectives.

Best wishes on your journey! And, don't forget to…

Always be *your* best!

Additional Information on "Belief"

A recording of my presentation about "belief" is available on my website:

slyoung.com/power-of-belief

Appendix:
Belief: An Underutilized Tool[8]

There are many life lessons taught every day, such as ways to deal with others, subject matter expertise, and learning basic survival skills. However, there isn't enough time allocated to teach individuals about the power of belief. This is surprising because belief is often a cornerstone of success. Moreover, if individuals don't believe in themselves, then the reason that others should believe in their activities or causes might not be as great.

Belief is a thought, feeling, or an internal drive that can be used to overcome an obstacle, advance toward a goal, or move beyond past challenges... sometimes despite overwhelming odds. Belief isn't required to move forward. Although, it's an important tool to help summon the energy to persevere during difficult moments or challenging times. Furthermore, the biggest benefit of possessing belief is that it supports something that is significant to someone, even if nobody else agrees with it.

Belief is something that is true to an individual, very personal, needs to be developed, and can be a

[8] Young, S. L. (5/12/14). Belief: An Underutilized Tool. Retrieved from http://www.slyoung.com/belief.html on 6/15/14

powerful tool for personal development. It's also a characteristic that can help individuals move forward, solve an issue, or to achieve a goal. Nevertheless, everyone doesn't have belief in themselves or may choose not to leverage their belief system to maximize their potential. Some reasons that belief might not be fully utilized are self-doubt, fear, or others' opinions. Notwithstanding, a significant reason that belief isn't used more often is that life experiences greatly influence an individual's ability to believe.

Things that happen during someone's lifetime effect their perspective and outlook. If an individual has had positive experiences associated with their beliefs, then their outlook is usually more positive. Conversely, if an individual has had bad experiences associated with their beliefs, then their outlook might be more negative. Although, a single bad experience won't always impact someone's outlook, unless an individual learns to SEE; that is, the individual experiences a (S)ignificant (E)motional (E)vent.

Once an individual begins to SEE, there is a realization (temporary or long-term) that something that was once believed to be unimportant is actually important or something that was believed to be important might not be as significant.

There are several components of belief:

- concept – an individual envisions a way to accomplish a task, activity, or project, which doesn't need to be fully understood for an idea to be developed

- consideration – something is evaluated as a possibility, but hasn't been selected as a viable option

- convenience – something that is used, done, or believed only if there is a potential benefit to an individual's position, situation, or desired outcome

Oftentimes, belief might not be used sufficiently because of a lack of confidence, questionable arrogance, or a negative roadblock. Therefore, belief must be developed and maintained to achieve an internal balance that will support their goals, which includes an ability to be positive in their actions, to not be confident in a condescending manner, and to prevent any self-defeating activities that might prevent themselves or others from making forward-progress.

Belief can be a challenge because no matter the amount that someone wants something to be true. There aren't any guarantees that a belief is correct, achievable, plausible, possible, reasonable, or viable. As a result, belief requires faith in something that (many times) cannot be proven to be achievable or attainable at the time it's pursued.

Other challenges with the development of belief are that individuals:

- have doubts
- don't have others' support
- aren't confident in their own capabilities
- have a need for approval
- haven't solidified their belief
- have a fear that prevents a pursuit of something that might be true

Belief helps to provide energy to complete something that someone wants to achieve. However, anyone who doesn't believe in something that is thought, done, or pursued can give-up long before the desired outcome is achieved. For this reason, individuals must understand that belief isn't required to accomplish something; although, belief can be a significant factor between experiencing success or failure.

Activities that can help develop belief:

- Work on a dream despite fears, which sometimes requires moving past personal limitations and barriers to develop an idea or to achieve a desired outcome.

- Consider an idea to be in progress and build on it.

- Act as if there isn't a possibility of failure.

- Continue to be self-motivated, even if there are setbacks.

- Minimize doubts and worries to maximize opportunities for success.

- Learn a lot from each effort, even if the outcome isn't as desired or expected.

Beliefs might not always be realized. However, individuals who don't pursue positive beliefs can limit their opportunities and options, along with minimizing their possibilities for a better future for themselves and others.

Remember… no matter the length of your journey, always be your best.

Appendix:
Getting Past I or You Can't[9]

There are times that you might think something isn't possible because you don't believe it, or others have told you that it's not possible or right for you. These are the moments that individuals must ask themselves: Is this _really_ the right thing for me? Others can provide guidance; however, you're the only one who can answer this question for you.

A few points to consider:

- An individual won't move forward toward a goal until there is a readiness to TEE-OFF; that is, an individual is ready to use their **T**ime, **E**nergy, and **E**ffort **O**n **F**ulfilling **F**antasies, as success isn't based on others' considerations, but instead on your considerations and actions.
- An ability to reach a goal, to persevere, or to achieve success begins with having and pursuing a dream.
- Develop a vision that will help to guide you toward the realization of your dream.

---

[9] Young, S. L. (3/2/15). Getting Past I or You Can't. Retrieved from http://www.slyoung.com/getting-past-limitations.html on 4/18/17.

- Associate with individuals who have higher aspirations and are 'actively' working toward or have achieved success. This can help you to maintain a positive focus toward a goal.

- Maximize your belief by taking action to achieve your goals, which is an important factor to achieve success, as it's almost impossible to accomplish anything by only talking about it.

- Understand that you're capable of doing much more than you might think, which will sometimes require a change of environment to fully connect with an experience.

- You're responsible and accountable for the outcome and consequences of your actions; be proactive and take ownership of your journey.

- Take a chance to do something you want because that choice can lead to unexpected journeys and outcomes (for yourself and others).

Guidance to achieve success:

- You must <u>believe in yourself</u>, even if nobody else does. It doesn't matter if things are bad at a moment; you must continue to believe that it's possible. Don't allow yourself an easy way out!
- You have the <u>power of choice</u>. If you get distracted, frustrated, or start to have doubts, use a pep talk to convince yourself that whatever you're working toward is still possible to achieve. This motivational dialogue will help to drive your ability to continue to make progress toward a goal.
- You must <u>be resilient</u> because challenges are a part of life. An ability to move forward despite past challenges is the difference between those who are successful and those who could be.
- You must <u>be persistent</u>, as this will demonstrate commitment to achieve your goal(s).

Life might not happen as you want, but there's always value in the pursuit of a positive journey. This is a major reason that an ability to achieve success is directly related to your attitude, beliefs, desires, choices, perseverance, and resilience. Therefore, will you use all these tools to help create the best possible you?

No matter the length of your journey... always be your best![10]

---

[10] Young, S. L. *Getting Past I or You Can't*. Simple Steps Real Change Magazine, 12/29/14. Online.

Appendix:
Are You Really Who You Think You Are?[11]

Individuals often rush through the world to complete activities each day to get through their daily lives; many times, running so fast that there isn't sufficient time to slow down and ask: Who am I; what am I doing; am I really who I think I am?

The last question "Am I really who I think I am?" is a question that I never thought I would ask myself. However, once some impactful moments arrived, I was forced to ask myself the other questions: Who am I; what am I doing?

It's sometimes said that opportunities are missed because someone isn't actively looking for something that's wanted. Although, if an unexpected event, choice, or outcome occurs, these moments can sometimes force an individual to stop, take notice, and sometimes change direction. It's in these moments that an individual often learns to SEE; that is, an individual experiences a (S)ignificant (E)motional (E)vent that forces a self-examination of their own reality. Then, after experiencing growth by learning to SEE, individuals sometimes begin to

---

[11] Young, S. L. (5/12/14). Are You Really Who You Think You Are? Retrieved from slyoung.com/who-are-you on 5/15/14.

ask themselves tough questions about the things that are or aren't believed to be.

These reflective questions (related to an individual's decision making) are based on three perspectives:

- Mental – decisions made based on thoughts about the elements under evaluation, such as the factors of, the considerations about, and the impact of an individual's choices. These decisions can be more difficult due to over-thinking, analyzing too much, or being convinced to believe something that isn't in alignment with an individual's beliefs

- Emotional – choices made based on an affecting response can cause a decision to be adversely impacted due to heightened sensory stimulation. These decisions can challenge an individual's ability to distance their feelings from external stimuli

- Spiritual – the mental and emotional perspectives can cause an individual to toil over their life's direction, because an individual's activities normally reflect their spirit and core beliefs. Moreover, an individual's core beliefs are often used to minimize opportunities for their mental or emotional perspectives from unnecessarily overriding their values

Any individual who uses the convenience of a situation to justify any action and/or behavior that doesn't align with their supposed core beliefs must question the conviction of their beliefs... as core beliefs aren't situational. However, there may be times that an individual's core beliefs are redefined based on new discoveries, corrections to previous opinions, or purposeful decisions to change their viewpoints. Despite these potential adjustments, core beliefs aren't as fluid as opinions which can change rapidly from one moment to the next.

In training for my professional career, there was never a conversation or a consideration about the possibility that I might need to make decisions that would cause me to choose between standing firm in my beliefs or being a party (willing or not) to questionable and/or unethical activities. Furthermore, none of my extensive training prepared me for the heart-wrenching decisions that were required to choose between remaining at a job and a conflict with my core beliefs that might impact my earning potential.

Appendix:
10 Lessons to Overcome Misguided Limitations[12]

Individuals can be quick to place limitations on someone's thoughts, ideas, capabilities, or potential. These limitations aren't always related to an individual's ability but instead by the limitations communicated and placed on them by others. These types of misguided limitations can cause individuals to not achieve their potential or miss opportunities for themselves, others, and society.

Lesson #1: Success requires tough decisions, even if the outcome can't be imagined at that moment.

In tenth grade, my principal directed me to leave high school after failing 6 of 7 classes. Prior to this direction, the administration didn't offer me any assistance to resolve my learning challenges. Nevertheless, during my adolescence and academic crisis, I decided to remain in school at a time that it would have been very easy to leave.

Lesson #2: The ability to make an 'active' choice is the cornerstone to being accountable and responsible for changes that might improve your

---

[12] Young, S. L. (9/10/14). 10 Lessons to Overcome Misguided Limitations Retrieved from slyoung.com/overcome-misguided-limitations on 4/8/17.

future.

It was difficult for me to remain in high school to receive my diploma. However, I knew that I had to make some difficult choices and changes to have a chance to maximize my future success.

Lesson #3: Don't let anyone make you believe that your options and potential are limited. If you believe it's possible, then give it a try. The worst thing that can happen is that you won't accomplish your goal, but there's still value in the journey.

During my senior year of high school, my dreams of attending college were dismissed by my guidance counselor who told me that I wouldn't do well as a college student. My counselor placed limitations on my potential versus providing guidance for me to begin forward-progress to achieve my goals.

Lesson #4: Don't be afraid to pursue your dream(s) because failure at a moment isn't a failure of your life or a representation of your value --- now or in the future.

After graduating high school in the bottom 8% of my class, I pursued my dream to obtain a college degree. Unfortunately, after a situation with an uncaring professor and bad personal choices, I would subsequently leave two colleges with a dismal academic record.

Lesson #5: Don't extinguish a dream because it wasn't previously successful. Failure in the past doesn't mean that a dream can't be realized in the future --- even if it happens in a way that wasn't originally imagined.

My initial pursuits of higher education didn't turnout the way I expected. However, a few years later, I decided to return to school after achieving some professional success and working with individuals who wanted success, too.

Lesson #6: Past performance isn't indicative of future success or potential. Success starts with personal belief that something is possible. If you don't believe, then others might not necessarily support your cause.

My grades were awful, I wasn't sure that I could complete college-level work. Also, I didn't believe that anyone would give me an opportunity to prove differently given my past academic performance. However, I believed that I was capable of more than my past indicated.

Lesson #7: The front door isn't always open;

therefore, individuals should seek other entry points. The ability to achieve a goal is oftentimes a test of commitment, which is directly correlated to the things someone is willing to give-up and the effort expended to achieve an objective. This is important as things that are truly wanted are done for a purpose and sometimes for passion; otherwise, individuals might quit long before an outcome is realized.

I was admitted to the American University after proving that I could complete college-level work via its non-degree program. After receiving my undergraduate degree from American, I wanted more success. However, I wasn't sure if I could give any more of my time, energy, and effort.

Lesson #8: Achieving goals and objectives requires dedication and sometimes creative solutions. At times, individuals don't achieve their potential because perceived barriers are seen as absolute limitations; instead, barriers should be considered challenges to an individual's capabilities, creativity, and commitment to seek options to minimize roadblocks to achieve future success.

My dream to obtain a graduate degree wouldn't be surrendered without a fight. Therefore, I researched information to maximize my chances to be admitted to another competitive program at The George Washington University. For a second time, I used an indirect process to achieve a desired outcome.

Lesson #9: Others can identify capabilities in someone that might not otherwise be considered. Sometimes individuals limit their potential because of doubts about their capabilities. Individuals shouldn't be afraid to try something because it wasn't part of their original plan. At times, the biggest successes are experienced due to unplanned choices, circumstances, or considerations.

After achieving my graduate degrees and excelling in corporate environments, an opportunity was presented to me to teach college students. Prior to this offer, an employee told me that I inspired him and identified skills that I never considered to be valuable.

Lesson #10: Belief in yourself (despite obstacles and objections) is a powerful component of success; however, options can be limited without a willingness to make a choice, take a chance, be committed to your quest, and be confident enough to give-up a little control.

I started to write solution-oriented material a couple of years ago to share my past struggles with overcoming educational challenges, workplace bullies/ethical issues, and life. The unexpected outcome of publicly sharing these challenges is my personal growth. I've learned that vulnerability (by sharing personal struggles) is a powerful tool to become stronger because of and not in spite of the disclosures.

Bonus Lesson: Today's effort initiates actions that lead to tomorrow's successes. Never give-up on the pursuit of your dreams, as moving toward an unknown destination can lead to unexpected outcomes that can change your life and others.

My recent sharing about my journey to battle depression and recovery from a near suicide has led to an unexpected journey (others seeking my advice and an invitation to be a contributor on the Huffington Post). Now, this student who was directed to leave high school in the tenth grade has an increased opportunity to help, inspire, and uplift many others through my writing.

Don't forget to never give-up and to always be <u>your</u> best!

About the Author

Dr. S. L. Young is an author, professor, career coach, former HuffPost contributor, founder of the educational non-profit organization "Saving Our Communities at Risk Through Educational Services (SOCARTES – socartes.org)," founder of the for-profit company "Beyond SPRH, LLC – beyondsprh.com)," and former host of "Beyond Just Talk with S. L. Young." The topics of his books include belief, communication, negotiation, time management, workplace bullying, ethics, overcoming challenges, and inspirational quotes.

In 2012, Dr. Young became an author with the release of his first book in the "It's a Crazy World… Learn From It" series.

Dr. Young graduated from the American University in Washington, D.C. with a Bachelor of Science in Business Administration (BSBA) degree in International Business with a marketing concentration. He also graduated from The George Washington University in Washington, D.C. with two degrees: Master of Business Administration (MBA) in Finance and Investments with a human resources concentration and a Master of Science (M.S.) in Project Management. In 2023, at Marymount University, he successfully defended his Doctorate (Ed.D.) in Educational Leadership and Organizational Innovation. The focus of his doctoral research was "Student Engagement's Impact on Academic Performance for Nontraditional Students in a Community College Environment."

In 2022, Dr. Young was inducted into and became a life member of The Honor Society of Phi Kappa Phi. In 2023, he was inducted into The Honor Society of Kappa Delta Pi. Additionally, he's a life-member of the professional business fraternity of Alpha Kappa Psi.

Dr. Young's professional career includes approximately fifteen years with Fortune 500 companies, including Bell Atlantic, MCI, Sprint Nextel, and various consulting engagements, in the areas of billing, customer service, engineering, finance, information technology, network security, operations, product development, and software quality assurance.

Dr. Young, for nearly fifteen years, has taught a variety of classes (i.e., Introduction to Business, Entrepreneurship, Business Communication, Marketing, Small Business Management, Organizational Behavior, and Principles of Management at the Northern Virginia Community College. He has also taught at Marymount University for over three years.

In 2012, Dr. Young created SOCARTES to share life and business lessons with individuals in opportunity "at-risk" communities. Through his work with this organization, he created additional pathways for him to give-back to and make meaningful connections in various communities.

Dr. Young's passion to help others is fueled based on his abilities to excel academically and professionally. These accomplishments occurred after being directed to leave high school in tenth grade, graduating in the bottom 8% of his high school class, and leaving several colleges prior to becoming actively engaged in the process of learning. These experiences drove his desires to tirelessly help others in meaningful ways and various environments.

In January 2015, Dr. Young launched Beyond SPRH, which provides solution-oriented services to help individuals and organizations to maximize output potential.

In 2018, Dr. Young received special recognition for his work to educate an incarcerated population. The first was the Martin Luther King, Jr. Drum Major Innovative Service Award from the U.S. Department of Education for Faith-Based and Neighborhood Partnerships, in collaboration with the White House Initiative for Educational Excellence for African-Americans. The second was the Distinguished County Service Award from Volunteer Arlington (a program of the Leadership Center for Excellence).

Dr. Young is driven to share his knowledge that leads to developmental opportunities (especially for underserved and marginalized communities). Through his authentic lived-experiences overcoming challenges, Dr. Young works tirelessly to inspire others to overcome challenges and pursue their dreams, too.

<u>Dr. Young's published works:</u>

- Above Expectations – My Story: an unlikely journey from almost failing high school to becoming a college professor

- Bullies… They're In Your Office, Too: Could you be one?

- Choosing To Take A Stand: Changed me, my life, and my destiny

- Ethical Opportunity Cost: It's a matter of choice

- It's a Crazy World… Learn From It:

  o Part I – Taking Care of Me

  o Part II – Moving Forward

  o Part III – Keeping It Going

  o Part IV – The Journey Continues

- Management Spotlight:

  - Belief

  - Communication

  - Critical Thinking/Thick-Skin

  - Negotiation

  - Time Management

  - Workplace Bullying

- Soft Skills Development:

  - Belief

  - Communication

  - Critical Thinking/Thick-Skin

  - Negotiation

  - Time Management

- Turning Darkness Into Light: Inspiring lessons after a near-suicide

www.ingramcontent.com/pod-product-compliance
Lightning Source LLC
Chambersburg PA
CBHW071221280526
45787CB00002B/752